From the Domain of Arnheim

By the same author

Poems
Seventeen
Catacomb Suburb

Criticism
Triumphal Forms
Conceitful Thought
An edition of Milton's *Paradise Lost*

From the Domain of Arnheim

Alastair Fowler

Secker & Warburg
London

First published in England 1982 by
Martin Secker & Warburg Limited
54 Poland Street, London W1V 3DF

British Library Cataloguing in Publication Data

Fowler, Alastair
From the Domain of Arnheim.
I. Title
821'.914 PR6056.0/

ISBN 0-436-16180-X

Printed in Great Britain by
Redwood Burn Limited
Trowbridge

Contents

Acknowledgements

Acknowledgements are due to the following, where some of the poems first appeared:

Akros, Ambit, Lines Review, New Poetry 4, The Scotsman, The Scottish Review, The Times Literary Supplement.

The Dutch School

The first lesson's a place, interior,
Familiarly Dutch, almost removed.
Imperial lilies are going, columbines
Fly from miraculous glass jars
And antique vases. Wheatsheaf bouquets
Or frothing loose cascades of tendrils
Is all the same. Even the yellow roses go
That van Huysum waited a year,
Or the pinks that Rachel Ruysch found time
To paint – a specialist after her tenth.
But children have no time for still lifes;
Eat too quickly to think of thinking
About not interrupting the Flannan feasts.
They lack the sadness for extended meals
At tables groaning with particular clocks
Quiet between ticks, and ponderous lobsters
For the lightest breakfast piece. Why hang about
The edge, dangling skin from the quick
Of a glistening lemon, just because it falls
In serpent loops? They do not care
For apricots bruised, for important flies
Regarding themselves in mirrors of grape.
They never think how the fruit has been felt
By someone living, someone dead.

What School Is This?

I couldn't make out what building I was at.
The height and shaping spoke:
A mansard roof that caught
And still defeats the eye's anticipation
Of height. (Look your fill at slopes less quick.)
Dormers that alternated with *oeils-de-boeuf,*
Blank, perplexed, staring from brows of lead.
And all raised up to view on crisp entablatures:
A sight for eyes. But those
Conflicting orders! Cyclopean piers
On an unnegotiable base;
And rusticated coigns
Without a figure in their vermiculations –
Nothing you could have put your finger on
To trace it out, if they had been in reach.
These monstrous blocks: how could they possibly go
With the arcade that frailly clung on to the wall?
Or the useless windows, gratuitously featured,
All broken pediments, complex eloquent forms.
What was the place? It was
A school for the blind.
                                        There seems not very much
To set against the evidences. Unless
This silken scratch, which distracts from the ocean's roar
Inside the imagined shell.
One of the Newtons is rubbing the smoother stone,
The rainbow-coloured one
He always failed to see.

The Great Wall

Here lies the wall, the stone-and-brick-scaled wall,
Once pompous-endless-snakelike, it liked
To crest each hill: to front from a hill above,
Turning each fact by higher courses in turn.
Foreshortened by great distance, its countering stance
Looked like tacking from side to side for ever
Continually, continuous from tower
To tower. But long defences tired defenders
Gripped by a fear of ladder ends; the snake
Lost its grip on the tail. Now the wall
Has met its end, somewhere in Shansi province.

Advice on the Cretan Labyrinth

It goes like this. Familiar errors rouse
The sense of locality; which leads you to feel
For scale and age, until you catch the thread
And go in circles to where they circle in.
By all means try avoiding. You can avoid,
Even, avoiding trying. You may cut short
The way or just lengthen; but you will end
(Let's face it) tracking the spiral right to the end.
Clear recognition now will let itself slip
Through doubtful visions and come to certainty.
Of course you can still prevaricate, deny
There is a centre, even, and the nearer you come
Complicate all the more the simple route.
But then you'll have to meet him back to back.

Theseus Forewarned

After he knew the minotaur
He felt unease: a conqueror
Might do no more than this
And go famous to Dis.

But now the girls are tickled to know:
How did he find a way below
To where the monstrous life
Ran from his hero's knife?

"And have the honours been hard to bear
Since you breathed the last of mortal air,
That day when vapour clouds
Hung round the cave like shrouds?"

They expect enormous plans and boasts
And tributes to Ariadne, almost.
He tells the truth, but blended:
Their heroes must be splendid.

– Such as don't find the centre place
To be at best the interface
Or elemental phase
Of yet another maze.

Not that he didn't earn his feast.
But the minotaur may be the least;
And when the beast is dead
It's worse without a head.

Now deeper holes will smell and drain.
Collapse, and swarming heads and pains
In the winding gut, earth's sinus,
Will show the power of Minos.

"The intersection was always ahead
And much further than any thread.
At last 'the beast was dead'
Is all that can be said."

He went for Ariadne's sake
Not for the prizes he would take.
But now her yarn was spun,
Another skein begun.

What could he do but gently claim
A measure of success and fame?
Then watch, alert, in case
This was another place.

Minos Attends a Viva

Not to examine, they say,
Would be to fail; but it's hard
To pass this flawless day
Judging weeds.

It hurts to pity these souls;
And yet their tremulous blurts
Of bright through button-holes
Do not convince.

My fairest questions sound dark
And make a subfusc gloom
In equivocal vivas. Voices
Die, quiet mushrooms.

That stiff reluctance to plead
We must severely immure
And press with silence, grim,
Forte et dure.

Congratulatory Firsts
Will be best. "Would you care to end
With the bounds of the cell? Or discuss
Creation's bursts?"

When I see this rose again,
That kind no longer grown,
It will have blown.

Have done with crude selection:
Nature's is eased by death
Too soon for ours;

And who are we to judge,
Unless we can always tell
The greeny amaranth
From the asphodel?

But can we afford to dispense
With assiduity?
Mere fitness will not survive
The states we contrive.

Before going in: the sky:
The thing we allow to pass
As it passes by.

But wait. Between the blues:
That smudge one wants to efface . . .
Icarus, cheating the maze.
A borderline case.

The Speaker Meditates Before His Lecture

I'm fattening up, I think.
Really I shouldn't drink
Before my talk

So many largish bowls
Of smooth animal fat.
But they like their trenchermen
To be top-hole.

My clothes are studded intently;
My pelt is well-oiled and pure
(Feel to make sure).

I should be fully prepared.
Let no preparation be spared.
Find room for every prep.
Exhaust them all.

Like pigs under table we sit,
So long my legs will wedge
Against the edge.

I eat all on the carte.
The thighs (we are taught) were once
Well-educated parts
Given to gods.

Too far too soon they bow
"We should be glowing now;
But there's plenty of time."

I hear the chair pronounce
Apotheosis. Me.
The clapping may change its bounce:
Scramble along.

A moment's blade will reflect
On me, pouring unchecked
Unpurified stuff.

God Passing By in an Emperor's Undress Uniform

The clothing hides no emperor's face
That can be turned to us, effaced

Behind it. Or else that clever Moses
From his hide might've conjured up a gnosis

Through lattices of fingers (once he'd observed
The shadowy hand). That preserved

From sight what may be never obvious:
The light of true goodness, the nucleus

Of the splendid envelope. Unlike our own
Frontal occasions, the eternal aeon

Is grasped behind. In retrospect,
In retrospect we learn, to contradict

An age diminishing. Our gods,
Put off by foul conditions, frauds,

Atrocities, have withdrawn, or shrunk
To full-faced *putti* with fleshy shanks;

To assumptions of various orders; to clouds
Of gritty grisaille; to grubby crowds

As dark as their characters in Hebrew script.
Our fathers, who once were used to be gripped

Out of a cloud, high spiriting
In thick air, or with angels sporting

In the garden, are today thought touched
Merely by the sun, or strange, or brushed

Aside. Those fathers died before
We studied their spirits, their faces. We know

Too late the things to have asked, the elements
That could have traced angelic aliment.

They painted what they couldn't understand;
But we interpret colours in the sand.

The Bushel

I have ridden a cock horse like a bear's back
Furiously
All through the tumbling garden forest and fell:
Isaac Newton's own favourite pudding
Has comforted me.
I have emperored in triumph, beating all
The families at home.

The Great Mother has spread her loving lap
For me. Or standing
In a close mouth at the stairs to my lady's heaven
I have held the two terrestrial orbs astride
My holy hands:
Played up and down old Plato's ladder
And stood and held.

Leg over leg I have climbed the library stiles
Easily:
Inherited incunabula of queens
And read well into them such things as never
Yet were spelt
With key and hand by mortal writer of type,
For those unswaddled.

So when I sprawl and shake the earth by hand
And unknown flowers
Anthologize, sucking my merest soil
Into their blooms, I shall never then complain
Of short measure.
That I haven't studied all my life, there is
No way of saying.

Little Ones

They really make you tired don't they
just? Make you feel your age
don't they?

It's not so much the effort
of spending and getting and worrying:
what a lover once sweated about: dying
another turn each time he sweated and
punched her card again or sighed
with the care.

But they leave your hot tips
to cool and take a far insight
that you lost sleep for for granted,
carry it out for real easily and
prove it a dud.

Dead. It
wasn't that you thought you meant.

Unholy Dying

Billy crouches draws and fans
His hair-trigger finger gun
Prrffinnger: a ricochet.
It's his turn to show at length
How to be hit when you get it right
In the gut: he staggers, looks aghast,
Topples (wooden with pain), but draws
Himself about. Then quick the gun
From the top-secret boot holster.
Or he grabs heaven between the stirrup
And the mercifully deep grass.
Or waltzed around by whistled airs –
Force forty-five – falls.
The practice steps of various deaths.
He's too intent on practising all
Death's variations to grow up.
When will he hit on some way
To kid these details out of mind?

Presents

When they give clothes, it doesn't count.
Opening presents you count toys,
The ones you wanted: the rest is trash,
Embarrassing. A silver fruit
In the stocking toe or atlases of space
Or wooden spades must pale before
The gun, which is test-fired at once
To check for faults (only caps,
And quiet action). But the pure curve
Of handlebars dropped thus
Is the right image of Ammon's horn.
Another Christmas, the power to give
Is greater. Nasty Augustine,
To damn our gifts and give Santa the sack.
This year you choose half-acre rugs;
And half a car honks to the other –
Nothing's too much when you set up house
Permanently.
When you are head
Ask a wrist computer, or a handless watch.
Things often used may please the most,
And the wrapping counts as thought. You might
Have leisure to play with a musical box
Disgorging pills, or a paperweight
Of snake-stone fossil coiled. But now
Those toys are broken. And how can you
Sustain excitement longer? It's time
To open the last surprise of all:
The eye of Horus wrapped with love.

Presents and Presents

To Lady Hertford's eye it seemed blank space,
The Chinese wallpaper sent by the Prince Regent:
She cut some Audubon birds to sing in the wastes
Beyond its trees. The Empress Elizabeth,
More eccentric, thought the most splendid gift
A lunatic asylum. How shall I rest
Until each working girl is gifted with taste
More to her mind: finer, less commonplace?

Our Poems of Age

With us it looks a dying genre,
The elegy of middle age. We groan
At profound chances not taken;
At girls not; erudition that lies
Heavily useless now; or sweetness
Confusing, taking the flesh of remembered years
To lie with snow on leaves unstudied.
Or else we measure our declining light
Into the gloom of blurring organs:
Count down to the last Venetian jaunt:
And miss the friends who left early.
Add an almost sigh at the arduousness
Of surviving nights through endless ages
Of age. Drop a tear. And then a hint,
Sinister, of that final summons
(But none of having received it long ago).
In our dark kind, the trick's to contrive
To seem to look the worm in the tooth alive:
To bury the fear of bells that slowly
Tell dampened sobs that we shall never hear.
(The world will end, when we are gone.)
Well it's natural, half-way over,
To stop for a thoughtful lunch: to take the sun
At his best zenith. Our lives may never
Bring so much again. We look down
On twilight, up to cliffs of judgement,
From here. But why? Why not through other tracts
Of finality grateful and cool to sense:
Refrigeria to calm again?

Ours are years of respiration.
Now we have found our evident selves; we work;
And can begin to find the other,
Hidden. It's all down hill. And at the foot,
Plain as the grooves of a great launching,

A way opens, often and easily found.
We are better than half-way to completion:
The rest is in our scope, to make for life.
Of course, our features fail. But they
Were there before, and will not be forgotten.
How should anything be forgotten?
– When the swiftest snowflake imprints without a flaw
Glancing into an infant's eye to melt.

A child I used to know was playing once
On blaes paths in a summer garden
With a sky to last for afternoon years
Rounded blue. The flowers faded
And I was called indoors. But it ended well:
It was all right: he was home, my father.
He read to us from *Sinbad* and talked about souls
Until we laughed and had the giggles
At his unanimal notions, while he towered there
At his genie's height. I see the features.
They are different now; but they are still the man.
What could decay that information?

The sun that sets will show us greater suns:
Our poems of age should all be praise.

Rose

There will always be more
to say about roses.
The terrible thing perhaps
is, we should not love them
unless they changed –
unless they exhaled and filled
and swelled and wrinkled and gave
the moment the perfume took.
Fragility
can have nothing to do
with preserving of moments.
Some go
generously blown:
when the gale rises, rises,
we shall never see them again.

What could fill the space
after the rose? The one
is like another, yet not,
not the same, not this.
Silver, like porcelain,
like perfumed silk, reminds
only. It is hardly,
the rose, a fluted edge:
that, we could plot. It is graining,
soft with pleasure ingrained,
smooth to bite.

It must be before the rain
moistened, before the musk;
the budding perfect yet
the blooms all gorged and swagged.

Would a reconstructed rose
serve, that I could mistake
again? To think so saddens
its look. Forget that time.
This, this
is what penetrates my space.

Getting Ready

The practice boat is out in the dark
Roaring and going in spite of ice.

But you have to start with gradual starts.
Gradually. Slow. To start with, perhaps,
You may have your knees touching the floor.

On all fours, until you are ready
For real push-ups. Not many:
Not so many as to frighten the heart:
Ten, performed with true art.

These take you where you want to go.
There may be a time of higher achievement,
Briefly and with stretched exercitation;
But remember the pennies that see you through
(In case you lose the place, the count).

Methods of swing and body work
Make the rowers better together,
Or else their feelings gradually
Change (chained to the great sweep).

Later still, put fewer coins
Beneath your blurring moister eyes,
Straining across the ink stream;
Then fewer still, and fewer still.
It will seem easy with only two.

Mr Ruskin Chooses a Travelling Carriage

Mechanical requisites first: steady strength –
Poise of persons – easy rolling, and then
Stateliness to abash plebeian gazers.
The intricate high hopes! The complex joys
Of planning grand accommodations for triumphs!

Savour the cunning cellars under the seats,
Secret drawers below the anterior windows,
And highly invisible pockets, safe from dust.
– Half the comfort depends on a perfect fit
(Of fully-fashioned doors and windows too).

The pockets are easily accessible
To us by insidious slits. Let in
Under the lining pads. They underlie
The padded lining. And the necromantic valves!
More delicate repose solicits rounding

Of each corner, smoothly. And best have
A small seat for father, in case of storms.
These plans of imagined trips cost no unease.
The singing intervals and passes of Europe
Open out.
But it was not enough.

All we have dreamt of security is not
Enough. The courier still stationed behind
Continually whispers, and still the motto
Spells from the painted arms on the polished side:
Vix ea nostra voco. Next,

Or round the next corner, the hermetic sealer
Drives in his black trap; or others in hearses
Pulled by slow moving plumed mares.
Less: a two-wheeled cart would do the thing,
Baron Larrey's dripping ambulance.

And yet uncounted turns of earth remain,
With many journeys. We need to spend a lot
On a vehicle of quite another colour;
Which will take us out to see the whole world
With a first stage burn fierce to consume our fears
And launch us as far as Ruskin might have strolled.

Things

The same ariser never goes down again
Or wakens from sleep. And he forgets himself:

How, when you move house, the drawers deliver
Grinning snaps, or teeth that once were yours.

Mountains that seem belongings in the loft
Cover graves of selves, dusty and fluffed;

And an owner of shoes of mine easily lazed
And labelled sunnier days in Palimpsest.

But who was ever innocent enough
To wag those earwigged hats with crowns the size

Of church collection bags, or hope to collect
All Cape triangulars of every shade?

These child's drawings, out of his own head,
Dust-gathering here, have missed the distance point.

Our time with things is far too short to lose
A clue to old oblivions. That sphere,

Our Christmas tree's gold fruit, was a souvenir
From the country of sheep, a better or simpler world.

One room has room for thoughts of all of these.

Relative

No Rembrandt's mother's face,
It changed in its possession.
I didn't want to sit in her dark, hated
Going to hear the blurring cataract
And see the same stories told again.
But the last times of all
She was too home-trained to blame neglect.
Gentled. She had a migratory look,
All steep eyes and fine glass bone.
Her knuckle tugged and clung to make quite sure:
Tell me I'm not to die.
(The old promise to stay young was broken.)
If you'd seen you would have wanted to keep her going
In spite of age: age that I might have kept
Coming some time more slowly. She was lucid, though.
To think that that could disconcert.
The senses fade and seem to leave quiet;
So that we feel relief when the fluttering stops.
Then a flame I thought was out blazed up
Again, like the bedroom fire she used to light
To make the harmless shadows, when I was ill.
Tell me I'm not to die.
Oh she is wonderful, they said, considering.
Only considering; not remembering, like me
(But unlike her), her former judgement. Have parts
Of all living been mislaid as far?
Knowing less of herself she similarly clung
To sameness. Her mind remained.
Then something much more fugitive would stray
Along old bridle-paths long overgrown,
Until the words were lost, and then their sound;
Even the stories. Visits anthologized
Only the most familiar recensions.
In longer episodes I might have told her
Apart from the tale. Tell me I still may.

Another Beginning

For C.M.G.

A sickle cry along the wall of glen
Scratched a line; and our eyes
Flew from reading scrolls of mist to go
Up to the indisputable seriousness,
Up from the small deserted wood. Again.
There the harsh reminder flies further
Away than we heard the call:
A heron, gradually navigating.
It directs a long course,
An almost leisurely course,
Levelled into the north beyond the sky
That already glooms with dusk;
As if it has to sail a great departure
To pass the reaches of the furthest light
Before it can travel on to fetch the murk
Beyond all borders, the distances and wastes
Of next obscurity.
Somewhere a place may be stag-beetle black.
Something remains planted deep in the wound
Of the sound within that call: a barb remains,
A vital point that was left
Behind our speculation.
Out it carries: the magician's truthful cry,
Whose action is desolation,
Meaning worse than anything we thought.
We waste too long on those inherited conflicts.
The heron gives no reprise,
But takes its fadeless grey to places that continue
Increasingly remote. And now by supreme
And final attention we have to form
The auguries that that most difficult mage

In trouble himself would beat the air to shout.
Commencement was parcel of it.
Quick! Look alive. Call,
So long as the eye has not completely failed,
A word about beginning.
Even counting from now we are bound to take
Thousands of years and lives of men to fail,
If now is a moment late.
Tomorrow it will be bright, hard to credit
Mist, and the faint sound
(Remembered least by this)
May not be thought so harsh as I believe.

First Words

1 There

"There," is what I'll say when I'm there. "No more
Of that long art. Not one more final draft
For what I hardly thought I could engraft
Upon those languages, while I lived there:
This life of undivided thoughts. But the words,
The difficult cases! How I relished each find.
Now I may share, and needn't speak, my mind;
So you know my heart's there, with the words I made
towards."

2 The Things We Used To Say

But . . . before you think of going
Let us pass over the river and rest
Under the shade. How sweet
It is to rest. We shall have such sweet thoughts.
Why wait until you finish your problem?
Let it be solved: how tired you must be.
As for me, I will go in:
I could eat a Bellamy's veal pie.
To think what in the natural course
I shall have for afters.

Balzac asked after his characters.
Anaxagoras for a holiday
For the boys ("It grows dark, boys,
You may go"). And Bayle had his proofs ready
Corrected. But . . . Schlegel failed to complete.
Between the ninth and the tenth verse,
Chenier's was carried out. At the thought
Of Textor's list others have laughed
Their names on to it. Copernicus touched
His blind book.

Open the window, let us have more light
On those illustrious words, which speak
The last of earth. Remember:
It has all been very interesting. Now
Comes the mystery: I shall soon know
The grand secret, the great perhaps.
And yet . . . it doesn't signify.
Tired, very tired: I must sleep now:
How sweet it is to rest.
Take my last notes.

Taught half by reason, law gives weight
To death words, sayings meant
Almost absolutely
(There are no absolutes), as if
On darkness' edge the thing grows plain
(A fearful leap into the dark):
How grand these rays! I've had a good life
(Give me back my youth, my country).
Wonderful this death (I have been
A long way away).

Myself again, I hope I may steal
Enough from sleep and compromise
To find myself, rehearsing
The wooden ceiling, blue and white
With simple rosettes. Severn is there,
And I feel the leafage growing down.
– But to wish beyond the last words
Is to wish never to speak the last:
To stay like this dreaming here
Of nothing but earth.

3 Full of Pie

Nothing at all.
Absolutely nothing.
Not a single thing to do
Ever again.
Nothing to do at all:
Nothing
At all,
Unless I want to.
Very much.

4 From The Domain of Arnheim 0-7156-0536-4 to Eruna Elith

Dear Coridon,
Safe back, without an irreplaceable event,
In the old Domain. I never knew till this
Quite how secure we are. You mention leave. I should like
One of the quieter Augustan modes:
Perhaps the shaven lawns cut from the dubious wild
Will offer a prospect of knowing peace again.
The mission was bad: we ran some criminal risks. In fact,
Our chronicle-chart of moments held in phase
Is classified, still. But we got a perfect holoprint
Of a Morgan draft; and enough to reconstruct
A case of Eiswein, '75. Best of all,
They say, a nicely blemished Tiger tank.
"No finer copy of primitive armour has ever come
Into our hands." I'd hoped the profitable catch
Might just have been enough, with a sponsor's help, to fund
A human reconstruction. But then we slipped,
As you'll have heard. Not all my fault: my briefing was brief,
Thanks to the Syndicates of Committee Boards
On Priority Bills. What shame, to tune so near to the real
Quite uninformed except by the usual fear
Of being trapped before. (How did they ever live,
When every death seemed final?) Well, we missed
Our subject long enough to use the energy up
That would have made a cerebral print. Worse,
A glider pilot near was badly hit, and his crew
Were failing to get the bleeding stopped.
We could have told them how – by missing a souvenir
And facing the sponsors' military music.
Or else we might have planted some green inspiring thoughts
Of other Arnheims. The self-effacing causes
Were calculated out, although we were far from phase –
Until I made my blunder, monitored here.
They saw, all right. The eternal return of gods in machines.
Angels, they thought we were, powers to believe
Or not; but not for them to think of starting to learn

To become. We moved away, without a sign,
Ashamed, masters of time. I longed to have shouted a word,
However rough, that might, however little,
Have loosened that ancient knot. How no deficiency of power
Detains the unraised dead, but slackness of love,
Our selfish planning, etc. So there it is; and now
All I can add is another formal appeal
To you, as Convenor, Resources Distribution Group.

5 Aging

Who could suppose these few laconic hours
Express our mind? Cast it right back:
Call to it, say, one morning break;
A spiked playground with endless centuries
In which to choose the game, the first of scores:
Tig, tag, toe the mark, who's
My leader, follow my love, or knife. The hands
Are out to pick the sides by arithmancy
Of fist over fist. In the age when you start to draw
And settle rules for nails and granny steps,
Just when you fight your first and lose the round
But hope for return, meetings, even to fall
In love, already the roaring bell stuns
For silence. How begin to be resigned?

6 How You'll Find It

Let me explain.
You go into a room
And come out again
With what you meant
Undone.
But you won't go back.
And the ones in the room
Notice no one.

7 Snow Wreaths

This is the snow the falls were drifting to.
From grains of powdered heaven, motes of the eye,
Plumes have swanned down and smoothed pillows,
Putting the grizzled flower-beds to bed;
Until we are snowed up, with all found
For ever. But not snowed by things. There's time
For a double take of every gander's quill.
Every bit. Each conversation flake.
As they fall, the whitest cats may scan how many
Crystal chandeliers alight in a blink.
And for long ages I'm free to tell how I love
This part of you, and this, and this, and this.

8 British Guiana 4c. High Yellow. Pelure Paper

Our unrare lives were quickly used, and yet
Could seem interminable, to us:
We had, I suppose, a frustrated wish for scope,
For calm unaimed at human ends.
To kill our time we hunted paper squares
And stuck them, each in its place, in,
In albums, leather-bound domains of peace.
We were most rapacious for ships. A fleet
Of brigs you might have thought would be enough;
Or one of those fleuron frames
That Mather authorized – with his own hand,
It may be, struck. Not for us.
We rummaged in cupboards, rifled for more, bought
At auction, or from stock-books crammed
Too full. Greedy by night we planned to swell
And manage the sets in ranks by day
Of well ranged lines abreast. And we would have
Sails' promiscuities bulging tight,
Bound to the east: from palest tints
To carmine rose, shades of bluish and blush,
Deep blue, blue, garter blue,
Dark blue, livid, purple and plum; or else
Mottled or blotched, streaked or barred
Right to the perforations. Never enough.
And all the foolish blunders: the "1"
In "British", "italic *s*", or simply "unsigned".
We studied them, with rigorous pains,
In time that might have made amends, or solved
A crux in *Hamlet*. Ah, but that
Variant calculus! Building power, we shaped
Its ideal order into a wish
To have in store, gathered comfortably in,
The ultimate collection. Towards that,
All slow and taxing drudgery was slight.
Few then could even have catalogued
Our fleets. And yet we hardly dreamed, back then,

What we were doing. We even liked
To push the silly things about. If one
Failed to know its proper place
We'd warn it soundly (just to ourselves, of course):
"Get back in line my girl; you'd best".

Shadows of Shadows

The thing is to keep our warm balloons of air
In air above the garlands of the underwood
Of stuff, until they sail, misunderstood,
Over the tree-tops, to light on your path: they bear
On the wind physicians of a mind, or razors
Irrevocably meant (if they fly at all
Up, without flame or course: not hang, dull
Shabby leaves, fruitless to paraphrasers);
But since, at even its roundest, signifying
(By what can spell, or be made, but never be,
Freedom) means less than saying (whose life may serve
A sentence for uttered deeds), it's best to deserve
Freezing at Yule for a spring of prophesying
Golden nails to fix the thing you free.

A Story Perhaps

The People tell
But without smiling, of a pond'rous bell
By a long rope let down the Pit to sound . . .
(Cotton *The Wonders of the Peak*)

Maybe it's like the lying tale
Solemnly told but not believed
Of fathoming the Elden Hole
By dropping a ponderable bell
On a monochord to sound the pit.
Overhand, open hand
Between the double walls they let
It go, to clink against the crust,
And after a while
Thousands of fathoms underground
To hit. But every effort failed
To make the signal ring,
Budge, even. – Until the cord
(Plundered) easily came away
Without a hitch.
But (and this was the stopper) throughout
Its length (like foreign ogham script)
It had been made wonderfully fine
With many curious cat's-paw knots,
Stunners, shrouds and rope yarns.
Undisentanglable:
Good rope utterly spoilt.
It was a matter of cutting it up
in disgust, or else mulling it over.
Some people twist the looser strands
Still; bending the well known knots
Until they seem rare diamonds.

Or Sound

Perhaps a truth. It is a truth
That the bell that hums today
Inside the behemoth roar
Of gales that inflect the oaks
Is not a lighthouse bell.

But the long apple branches roll
With a breaker's widowing rush,
And blossom sails unset
On a moth-destroying tide
Higher than any shore.

Yet the sound is far away from loss;
And what it tells of a place
Beyond the earth it will be
Quiet to listen in:
Remember to tell again.

It comes on long prevailing winds
To where the fruit trees groan;
Where pruning and cutting recall,
And burning, from long ago,
To more than simple dreams.

The Fisherman's Wife

Offshore the hidden rocks
Are sharper than seems;
And harder than fishing boat
Can touch and stay afloat.

Three go down quick
Where nothing breaks
The green but crabs and flesh
And then more crabs and fish.

After a week the sea
Washes one
With sand all through its hair
Up on the shingle there.

Run and fetch her quick.
At the washing green
Hanging out his clothes.
When that is done she goes

And picks away the crabs
Frilling his wrists.
From a face unpicks what clings.
Those are his messed things.

Each crab she softly takes
And drops in a pail.
Then says to the fishermen
To put him out again
Lads: set him again.

Sorrows Bring Forth

How unaccountable, when I am hurt
Or lost in random dread or partly ill,
That I should discover any relief at all
In words. How could a poem change this hurt?
Desperate cures from a past screaming with hurts,
Obscure despairs, hard to read, which the dead
Laid out according to ancient forms as they said
How ill or null they felt: they still ease hearts.

Primordial horrors have lost force: mine will.
The vigours that threw down ramparts can set me up.
Those low and earthy works give timeless hope.
Restored by choice of the nearly lost, I fight
To make his poem in ways he never thought
True of a hurt that might have made him stop.

On Rereading an Early Love Letter

A star set down in cuneiform on clay,
Which flaring burnt to the dark and pulsing heart
Ten million times too faint for human gaze,
Could after seven thousand years relay
Its ancient flame by radio waves that must,
To those who read them in clear, recall that blaze
Before. But my best art can never show
How you have made, through all our life, my day.

Young and Blue

Not lions that lack and fangled whippersnappers,
But bright pink rhubarb, blood, warm bread, mown hay.
Wrinkles and deals, Jerusalem, ideas,
Virgins and fashions, in splinterfiery May.

Not school ties, hat, abuses, maids, or fogies,
But time-changed ruins, incunables, jeans and sages.
Legends of customs, alliances, ideas,
Velvet madeira, codgers, friends, or stagers.

Andrew Marvell's Complaint:
Homage to Chomsky and Lyons

Colourless green ideas sleep furiously;
But when false dawn restores the flesh that nightfalls fade
Her red and white awake in peace, luxuriously:
Arouse again a flesh-coloured thought in a green shade.
I simply ask that passionate love should be straightaway made –
And find? Her duplicity betrayed by enervation.
I hear my merely double-hearted thirst delayed
Coolly with "*Quadruplicity drinks procrastination*".

Exeat

Coming out of that small wood
Where I lay explaining for hundreds of hours and went
Excused, I stopped. The world looked about
Its worst. That was as much sky or shine
As I could ever hope. But where a sign
Might lie, the surgeon of trees would not:
Refused to pretend to know. To circumvent
The ordinary axe was commonly the line.
But I was out; we were all together out.

Forest Clearing

Why do we love a wood to have no end
But gloom into darker shade, a tone of void?
We ought to go in for the chance of stars, though pathless,
Or gaps with rides to interesting houses.
Even in sacred groves, we should be thrilled
To think that unbroken ranks of angel firs
Might somewhere thin at last, disguarding Eden.
But it seems we want to keep the guarantee
Of timber not to be felled for Paradise;
Wishing for rings of trees encircling us,
With a secret not to be found somewhere beyond.
– As if, when all was plain, it would evanesce.
We like a forest virgin, tenebrous,
Holding at length enormous promises.

For T. H.

Back from the street and through a close,
Dark and loud with thunder flags,
You went down the steps under the sea
Where greenish bottles of light were popping
In a doll's emporium, full of counter.
Facing, the reredos of glass:
Figures and columns of jars on jars:
Illuminated confectionery:
Mountains of caramels, comfitted close
And things buried in dark sugar.
Bon-bons and jujubes,
Jelly babies and liquorice tubes,
Tutti-frutti and fruit gums,
Barley sugar and sugar plums,
Lozenges and lollipops,
Berwick cockles and chocolate drops,
Mint imperials and peppermints,
Strawberry pralines and rhubarb rock,
Fierce horehounds and tiger pillows,
Honey-brown humbugs that caught your nose
And sandy ginger candies that snapped.
Not to touch. You cleared your throat
Until Teenie heard and shuffled through,
Wheezing and rolling, overall bulging
Round as a big dragée, to find
A cough pebble frosted white
With a black inside. Staggering with jars
She would pour the carefree scoopfuls out
On to her true and brazen scales,
Which TURN WITH THE ONE-MILLIONTH PART OF LOAD.
She must have loved me, been truly mine,
To give me all those sucky sweets.

Continuity

There was this poet who thought we'd never come
To the very end, ever, of the whole line.
Always Atlantis would improvise a way
Of starting again; or we'd learn by our mistakes
How to make more (or fewer), and when we must
Accept new forms, how to accept new forms.
Just before oil gave out, fusion would solve,
In the nick of – "Time will be up at last
For Earth? Well then, we'll take to space (if not
Our bodies) our ghostly selves in man-machines."
Now he is merely dead. And in his place
I live, continuing, constructing him.

In Arcadia

. . . of recovering it dwindles away.
Sometimes the going is all uphill,
The outside chance lying in words
Of a tribe that Humboldt's parrot heard.
Our undertaking's remnant now
Is the search (apart from minding the sheep)
For a monument lost in perpetual woods
That it may not fall to us to find,
Nor any of our generation to find.
Nor even to know we haven't. But this
At least is not the place to know;
Although it is late to hit on a way
Among the leaves so wildly blown
To keep continuing to look.
At best we hope to stumble on,
Not find the lettered stone on maps
Beneath these volumes of leaves. And still
Chattering without interpreting goes on
Against the oceanic hush
Of the darkening wood. Have we the time,
If earlier wanderers left the cherub
And the winged phrases legible still
Through the blackened moss? – have we time to learn
To make it out, the inscription? Think
How much it took to set the stone
Up for us, here, where the long hill . . .

Resiting the Obelisk

The legend is false: no special words explained.
When slackened ropes made leverage fail and men
And horses fail to pull, when the monolith
Tottered, no timely voices intervened
Obelizing the silence on pain of death
To shout *Water the ropes!* Sinews twist
And ooze; draft horses' buttocks cleave,
Sweating, and Ra begins again to rise.
Only a disafforested cry, a tone,
Signals the gift of life: the quarrel
In its great machine at the city's heart is eased
And the ordered rest can sound its unison note.
We thought the age for gods to be historic,
In which the nameless obelisk rises again.

A World on Wheels

It's a funny world;
But no one's laughing
Fit to burst out.

It's a rum world:
So drown your sorrows
And have another.

It's a proper bastard,
Just like our fathers':
A right mother.

It's a mad world –
All insane,
No asylum.

It's an all sorts world.
Needing sorting,
Some of them.

The Poem We Are Going Towards

Sometimes I write what comes, easy as lying,
Much to my mind. Perhaps regret would fill
An octave? Easy as leaves on the tree it's sighing
Just as I feel. But feeling can heave away
Without a sigh-clogged word remotely flying.
The kind of poem I am afraid to want
Would start with saying and do far more; trying
To work to make what's not yet there to be felt.